RISE
UP!
POEMS OF PROTEST
POEMS OF PRAISE

Andrew Wilbert Fitz
Mari Fitz-Wynn

Faith Journey Publishing

To the mothers and fathers of all countries, and to the advocates of Christian peace everywhere this work is sincerely dedicated.

"A word fitly spoken is like apples of gold in settings of silver." (Proverbs 25:11)

"Let the words of my mouth, and the meditation of my heart, be acceptable in thy sight, oh Lord, my strength, and my Redeemer." (Psalm 19:14)

"O that my words were new written! That they were printed in a book! That they were graven with an iron pen and lead in the book forever." (Job 19:23-24)

-Andrew Wilbert Fitz

Rise Up! Poems of Protest, Poems of Praise
Copyright © 2022 by Mari Fitz-Wynn

All rights reserved. No portion of this book may be reproduced, stored in a retrieval system, or transmitted in any form or by any means—electronic, mechanical, photocopy, recording, or otherwise—without prior written permission of the publisher, except as provided by United States of America copyright law.

Published 2022 by Faith Journey Publishing, LLC
Printed in the United States of America
ISBN: 979-8-9858168-0-8

Cover design by Leah Morrison

For information, contact:
Faith Journey Publishing, LLC
contact@faithjourneypublishing.com

Scripture references are from the King James Version of the Bible unless otherwise noted.

CONTENTS

Foreword
Acknowledgments
Author's Introduction

Creation and I
Fearfully and Wonderfully Made

Do You Wonder Too?
Prejudice and Prayer

Let Us Now Lament
George Washington Carver: "God's Scientist"

Find Something New
Dead Soldier

The Prayer
Jesus

Water
Apostrophe to Wind
Nature's Symphony

The Prisoner
Upside Down

Mental Architecture
Cosmic

Hands Up! A Litany
Pleasures

Afterword

FOREWORD

RISE UP! Poems of Protest, Poems of Praise by Andrew Wilbert Fitz and Mari Fitz-Wynn calls the reader to "Incline thine ear unto me and hear my speech." Andrew Wilbert Fitz, one britches leg deep out of the enslavement of his family understood how to theorize about a world that did not love him back through voice, memory, vision, and agency.

Through his religious stance, he echoes the relationship between mourning, eulogizing, and lamenting. Poetry written long ago become his granddaughter's litany of praise for his acts of illuminating truth. "Let now our lament fill the heavens" was not necessarily what he wished for his granddaughter poet Mari-Fitz Wynn to find herself inside of, "how long shall prejudice be mixed with prayer, how vain this thing called prejudice we dare to mix with our worship and fruitless prayer."

Mari Fitz-Wynn, keeper of the family stories and specifically the agent of witness for her grandfather's poetry utilizes the text of her grandfather's poems and creates a call and response with her own poetics to reimagine how lamentation is also a form of gratitude. There is powerful eulogy present as a reaction to the loss of humanistic codes and values. The granddaughter becomes the documentarian using family artifacts and documents as primary sources to illustrate and affirm parallels between the personal belief system and it's influence on the outside world.

The grandfather's work in this process becomes a beacon lighting a poetic path homeward not just for the granddaughter but for those who read this collection and are reminded of all the rich connections and possibilities of kinship, reclamation, creativity, and revolutionary love. This poetic duet is an example of how the ancestors continue to hand us seeds from the depths of dark pockets of despair knowing that we are the air of their breath and the oceans of water their seeds need to grow and manifest.

Andrew Wilbert Fitz also whispers through ancestral veils a warning that the flesh of these present-day matters is still dangerous as he implores the future, "Save us from mundane birth… keep us free… let us stay unborn." His words throughout document, historicize, and agitate us all to think critically about issues of our collective humanity that are relevant to society while appreciating the poet's use of poetic form, language, and imagery.

Mari Fitz-Wynn boldly embroiders the framework of her grandfather's poetry through her dedicated stewardship throughout the process of sharing his early and brave protests of social injustice, imperfections of the spirit, and his powerful stance on the power of utterance. Perhaps, nothing has changed much in our eyes, but the blend of the grandfather's traditional art form and the granddaughter's delicate orchestration of economizing language is a gift that sometimes is fraught with pushback when avant-garde writers and artists mix the old and the new.

These poems are emblematic of the reality that many things that cause strife and sorrow are also the things that cause an uprising in the spirit. The pages of RISE UP! Poems of Protest, Poems of Praise is a metaphorical offering of a wellspring of solidarity that our world needs. These pages help us drink fully of the possibilities of laughter knowing that weeping dehydrates the body; reminding us that we are the water bearers of hope.

Jaki Shelton Green
North Carolina Poet Laureate

ACKNOWLEDGMENTS

To my grandfather. Without the inspiration of his poetry, it is likely this book would not exist. Thank you for allowing us into a few of your innermost thoughts.

To my aunt, Aleane Fitz Carter. Thank you for answering my endless questions about your father and our family.

To my children. You've already poised yourselves to take the baton of your legacy and run.

To Suzanne Rhodes. Who started this project as my amazing, patient editor, and ended the project as the newly named poet laureate of Arkansas.

To Jaki Shelton Green. The poet laureate of North Carolina, and poet extraordinaire. Thank you for believing in this project.

To Leah Morrison. Thank you for letting your creativity flow to produce a wonderful book design.

To Kimball Honoré McNeal for her countless hours of book formatting and layout.

And above all ...

To the Everlasting God, the Lord, the Creator of the ends of the Earth, thank You for breathing life into this work.

INTRODUCTION

My great-grandparents, Joseph and Louise Fitz, were born in the "evening" of slavery and worked on a plantation in St. Augustine County, Texas. Two years after emancipation they found out about their freedom and migrated west with the many freed slaves who became known as the Exodusters, eventually settling in Kansas.

My grandfather, Andrew Wilbert Fitz, was the middle child of eleven siblings. He was a brilliant man: an inventor, a poet, an activist, and a pastor, but I did not know him well. As a small child, I often took trips to my grandparents' house in rural Iowa. I couldn't see the neighbor's houses on either side—my grandparent's house sat back miles from the road. My favorite place was the big screened-in front porch where my brother and cousins and I would play for hours on end, sheltered from the heat of the Iowa sun. My least favorite place, however, was the outhouse. In the dark, the path to the weathered building seemed to stretch out endlessly before me.

I remember grandparents who doted over me. As I was the youngest grandchild, my grandmother would welcome me back for my summer visit with my favorite dessert, peach cobbler, its buttery crust and the sweetness of fresh peaches letting me know how much I was loved. Most of all, I recall my grandfather's booming voice filling the walls with stern admonitions and joyous laughter. Sadly, that same voice was silenced from a stroke long before I knew the important questions to ask about his early life. I would have asked, what was it like growing up with parents who had only known the judgment and harshness of a slave master? Or, how did his family manage food, clothing, and shelter? Could they read? How did he manage to finish high school and attend college despite the challenges? Thankfully, many of his thoughts were captured by his pen and put into words. He published three poetry books and wrote countless poems that remained unpublished. That he was known among his peers as the "Protest Poet" shows he was always keenly aware of the countless social, racial, and class injustices in the world he occupied, and more so, he was unwilling to remain silent in the face of an unjust status quo.

His love of writing, social justice, and God's creation is part of my legacy. I am called to write. When I write I feel most connected to my grandfather. As writers we believe through the grace of God that our words change lives.

Were my grandfather alive today, I believe he would have initiated this idea, to join our poems together into one book, and speak out with one voice. Perhaps his works today would have a tinge of grief noting that the world he wrote about in his 1949 book *Poems of Protest* had changed little for his grandchildren and great-grandchildren. I also believe that juxtaposed with his disappointment would be the hope that the world he strove for would yet be.

My hope for republishing his poetry and adding mine to his work is that it will become an inspiration to all of us to bind beauty to truth and fix verse to the cause of justice.

Grandparents Andrew and Beatrice Maddox Fitz, at home in Omaha, Nebraska

CREATION AND I

I am part of all creation—
how it fills me with elation!
Forest, plains, gigantic mountains,
oceans, rivers, restless fountains.
Sandy deserts, constellations,
sight and sound that function ever,
cosmic bonds that none can sever—
all the forms of life that wander
everywhere, some here, some yonder.
Art and science, with short direction
enter life for my inspection—
everything with me has option,
all exist for my adoption.
Crown am I of all creation,
and, regardless of my station,
let me act with that distinction
free from custom and convention,
burdened not by stale tradition
and those things that slay ambition.

Let intelligence exalt me,

let constructive thinking guide me.

Thus I say with adulation:

I am crown of all creation!

-AWF

FEARFULLY AND WONDERFULLY MADE

Ochre, amber, ebony, sepia earth tones for earth skin:
I am fearfully and wonderfully made.
Long, short, kinky, curly hair for wonder's sake:
I am fearfully and wonderfully made.
Straight, flat, wide nose for freedom's fragrance:
I am fearfully and wonderfully made.
Thick, round, full, thin lips for words of hope:
I am fearfully and wonderfully made.
Big, piercing, gentle, curious eyes for searching out truth:
I am fearfully and wonderfully made.
Fisted, open, praying, reaching hands for grasping grace:
I am fearfully and wonderfully made.
Walking, running, protesting, standing on strong legs for justice:
I am fearfully and wonderfully made.
Beaten, broken bodies surviving for greater things:
I am fearfully and wonderfully made.
Gifted, challenged, curious, inspired minds set for eternity:
We are fearfully and wonderfully made.
Psalm 139:14   –MFW

Mari, her brother, and cousins. Mari third from right.

DO YOU WONDER TOO?

Billions of shimmering stars
create a lacy overlay
against a midnight sky
and I wonder...
Wild foamy ocean waves
spew forth centuries-old
sea glass and shells
and I wonder...
Frosty caps of snow
drape purple and blue
majestic mountain peaks
and I wonder...
Palettes of color
too wondrous to name
open and close the dusk and dawn
and I wonder...
Rough-hewn, spike-riddled,
blood-stained cross
stands starkly on a hill for all to see
and I wonder...

Stone-shut tomb
in deadly quiet amidst outrage
and clamor of spirits, lies empty
and I know,
the Creator of every wonder lives.

*"For by Him all things were created that are in heaven
and that are on earth, visible and invisible" Colossians 1:16*

−MFW

PREJUDICE AND PRAYER

"And have made of one blood all nations of men to dwell on the face of the earth, and have determined the times before appointed, and the bounds of their habitation" (Acts 17:26).

In these significant words the great Apostle Paul expressed the oneness of humanity to the contemptuous throngs of Athenians as he stood on Mars Hill expounding to them the teachings of the Messiah. The following poem is based upon the unity of peoples by the bonds of blood.

Spires pointing upward to the far-off stars—
bright Venus, Jupiter, and gory Mars:
temples magnificent adorn the earth
where much is preached of the cross and Virgin Birth,
where the masses hear sermons of what lies ahead
concerning the rising of the dead,
concerning Jesus dying once to save
impudent mankind from the eternal grave.
Yet here prejudice enwraps itself with prayer
the while imploring sweet relief from care.
Too, prayers are said for those in distant lands
by race and color-hating, haughty bands.
How long shall prejudice be mixed with prayer?
Of "one blood" wrote the prophets: do we care

if blood again masks the face of Mother Earth
while we ignore the Man of Virgin Birth?
How vain this thing called prejudice we dare
to mix with our worship and fruitless prayer!
How shall we to the Son of Man explain
why we His creed of brotherhood disdain?

                                                -AWF

LET US NOW LAMENT

Tears flow from our prayers,
repentance bows our head.
Our ears are dulled to cries for mercy.
We've winked at injustice,
turned our face from truth
and wrongly ignored strife.
Our souls' weariness becomes
the goad by which we now come
with sins piled higher than our heads.
We lift our hands yet higher to receive
that which we've often withheld:
forgiveness, grace and peace.
Let now our lament fill the heavens.
                              –MFW

Mari overcome with emotion after touring slave quarters at a plantation in Creswell, North Carolina. (Photo courtesy of Kimball Honoré McNeal)

DR. GEORGE W. CARVER— "GOD'S SCIENTIST"

He held the keys to Nature's paradise,
    serenely viewed them with inquiring eyes:
"This one unlocks the secret of the vine,
    and this one, secrets of the stock and pine.
This one discloses truths of Mother Earth
    that makes her to abundant crops give birth.
And here's the key to jewels found in clay,
    rare dyes and colorings to make life gay.
Now let us look on plants that men call 'weeds'
    and use them to produce for human needs.
Search now for cause of failure in the crops,
    or find the reason when production stops;
of Nature's agencies to make things grow
    to give the strength to live to all below.
Ah, the labyrinth of Nature, infinite,
    there is no end to my untold delight
in bringing forth to man the things you hold
    of priceless good for all: how you unfold
to me to whom creation's God exposed
    truths seldom to the mind of man disclosed.
Thanks for the spirit you have given me
    to look within. Thanks for each magic key.

Thanks for my choices to court humility
    not pride, nor arrogance, false dignity—
but rather stand as a soul from wondrous sod
    exalted by the wisdom of Nature's God."

("Semper novus quid ex universe"—
Always something new from the universe.)
                                  -AWF

FIND SOMETHING

that fans the flame,
no need to know its name.
Awaken the gifts of God within,
gifts of love and grace to spend.

In your pursuit, and in His time
if you will seek, know you will find.
Let Him reveal what's in your heart—
He'll give you a nudge, a joyful spark.

Yield to passion within your soul
then wait and expect the Spirit to blow,
to stir in you embers of boldness and zeal
and grant you resolve to do His will.

Feel the warmth that kindles within,
a yearning to reach those broken by sin,
a calling so loud you can't ignore
the cry rising from your heart's deep core.

A powerful flame no one can quench
with discouraging words or discontent.
Find the dream that lights your soul
and though it may seem impossible,

What God declares none can prevent
for in His will each life ascends.
He knows the plans He has for you
to give you hope, and a future too.

Jeremiah 29:11

–MFW

DEAD SOLDIER

Sleep, soldier, sleep, and raise your voice no more
in wrath at foes in sky, on sea or shore.
The battle for the truth and right goes on
while demon souls on earth dare hiss: Begone!
Away with justice, freedom for mankind!
Such enemies to good desires are blind
and value not the priceless blood you spilled,
nor that of millions ruthless war has killed.
Rest, soldier, rest, in folds of friendly sod,
await the trumpet sound of a loving God,
and then arise and tell your gory tale
of how your life was wasted in this vale
of tears and tombs, of grief and troubles rife,
and squandered years of futile human strife.
Expose the lies that ordered you to slay
your fellow man and brothers wrapped in clay:
tell of the heartless heads of governments,
the kings, the princes, and the presidents
who sent you forth to die for an empty cause
despising God and all His sacred laws.

Stay, soldier, stay beneath the troubled waves
where many sleep, like you, in watery graves
unmarked, unnumbered, where the living ones
cannot erect bold monuments to sons.
Once children, parents' pride, they played and sang
and laughed until the air with music rang.
Sleep soldier, rest, and stay until that time
when earth is filled with righteousness sublime.
Blessed with the fullness of Messiah's peace,
and minds from fear are given full release.

–AWF

THE PRAYER

Almighty God, please heed our desperate plea:
Save us from mundane birth and keep us free
From death prepared by man to slay his kind.
Deliver us from hosts, destructive, blind:
Save us from atom bombs, from victory
Recorded for earth's future history
Won at the cost of priceless, precious life,
Grave answer to all bloody human strife.
Deliver us! For destruction awaits
Our entrance into life's chaotic gates
Where man builds monuments to heroes dead
While living souls lack shelter, beg for bread.
Keep us from blitzkrieg, poison gas, and gun,
And smoke of lethal flames that hide Your sun.
Preserve us from the peril of the skies
Created by the hate that men's hearts prize.
In safety keep us from the waters vast
Mined with explosives and their deadly blast.
We, the unborn, the formless, let us stay
Beyond the womb until the war-less day.
Let us be victims of bold Onan's crime
Rather than die by war before our time.
Father of waters, planets, night and morn
We ask Your mercy—let us stay unborn!

–AWF

JESUS

His name is a complete sentence,
His name a complete prayer.
His name is the radiant solution
to every problem.
His name can resolve conflict.
His name brings peace into every storm.
His name is protection.

JESUS.
His name is music—
it's the sweetest melody.
His name quenches the thirsty soul
and fills the heart's hunger.
His name guarantees salvation.
His name brings light
when darkness surrounds.
His name is joy unspeakable.

JESUS.
His name Emmanuel
means He is God with us.
His name is perfect.
His name alone brings healing.
His name is altogether lovely,
magnificent, glorious.

                              -MFW

WATER

Mysterious, ageless, complete:
In you children wade with happy feet.
Water, conveying great ships from afar,
Guided by the mariners' compass and star.
Water, from clouds to earth, roof, and pane
Brings joy to children splashing in rain.
Water that fills oceans, brooks, and lakes
Brings fresh life to plains and halls of caves.
Water, reflecting both tree and star,
Water, reflecting seen things as they are.
Water, for surgeons, for artists, for cooks,
Pictures of water in glossy-paged books.
Water, the boon of mankind, slave or king.
Water, the power that binds everything.
Water, that washes the soil from the hill,
Water, that gambols and sings in the rill.
Water, that bore Noah's ark for many days,
That fashions the rainbow all people's praise.
Whether in pool, in pond, or sea,
Water, your presence fascinates me!
Baptismal water for souls seeking light:
Symbol of change from wrong to right.
Water, that gives life to seed and sod—water, eternal witness
of mighty God.

-AWF

Andrew Fitz, Student, Kansas State University

APOSTROPHE TO THE WIND

Universal messenger,
Let me be a passenger!
Let me be your guest and soar
To heights I've never known before.
Let me mighty oceans span,
Let me lofty places scan,
Let me travel as you sweep
Across the land and waters deep.
Let me watch you stir the seas,
Bow the arms of forest trees,
Skip across the desert plains,
And transport the drenching rains.
Turn the windmills everywhere,
Scare the wild beast from its lair.
Let me watch as ocean spray
Leaps from waves you tell to play.
Share with you your journeys far
To the realm of distant stars.
Skim above Mount Nebo's side
Where the noble Moses died.
Let your voice, oh wondrous wind,
Say, "You are my guest and friend!"
                              -AWF

NATURE'S SYMPHONY

Oh! The surprise when
 a sudden
summer breeze
 begins
a symphony—
the gentle sway
 among
the leaves soon
swells
 as
a broken twig, now a
baton
seems to tap tap
 keep
up the beat—
warbling
song floats through the air
 with
each bird joining
in
then right on
 cue
the rhythmic
 cadence
of cicadas
 rises
and swells to a rich

  crescendo—
the deep bass
of bullfrogs croaking
brings the undertone—
  frogs stretching
and leaping as
crickets chirp
the downbeat
and katydids
 sing—
each creature's
voice
 filling the
air
as each performs
 his part
in the symphony
and the
  dance.
       -MFW

THE PRISONER

Intelligence sat bound
while fierce foes stood around
conspiring avidly to keep her so.
Ignorance, the arch foe of man,
gloated over this drastic plan:
"The seeds of prejudice will quickly grow
when planted in each mind
of trusting humankind,
These simple, thoughtless hordes who do not know
in turn imprison all who think,
who from wells of knowledge seek to drink.
Let us shut wisdom's light to perfect our plan.
Confusion elevate!
Establish terror's state!
Abolish hopes of progress in all lands."
But cosmic law is firm:
It deals with star or worm:
It metes out justice as each thing demands.

–AWF

UPSIDE DOWN

Though we exalt Him
He walks beside us.
Though we bow to Him
He lifts us up.
Though we pray to Him
He prays for us.
Though we must ask Him
He already knows.
Though we fight alongside Him
His victory was won.
Though He is our King
His Kingdom's ours to come.

                        -MFW

MENTAL ARCHITECTURE

Out of the world's mental muddle and mass
truth gleams, prolific, all people to bless,
pregnant with wisdom that all may enjoy
life free from thoughts and acts that destroy.
Build in the mind your world of success,
make it replete with thoughts that inspire.
Make it a kingdom where color and race
are not stigmatized nor assigned certain place.
Build in the mind, then let it come forth,
your visualized state of true godly worth—
progress within makes progress without.
Believe, embrace faith, eliminate doubt!
The universe holds all the matter you need—
visible solids, liquids and seed.
Build first within, then build without,
and practice this rule: be sincere, be devout:
Know that the unseen, the visible holds—
know that each thought the visible molds.
Build in your mind and let that world be
a shrine of the truth, the happy, the free,
a castle of courage where thinking is taught,
constructive, progressive, with good motive fraught.

Build in your mind the things that give birth
to better conditions for mankind on earth.
Build in your mind the brotherhood law:
kind acts will follow its use without flaw.

–AWF

COSMIC

The universal will is cosmic law
forever functioning devoid of flaw.
Each thought is part of the universal plan:
He who enslaves the mind enslaves the man!
                              -AWF

HANDS UP!—A LITANY

"Also, our enemies said, 'Before they know it or see us, we will be right there among them and will kill them and put an end to the work.' Then the Jews who lived near them came and told us ten times over, 'Wherever you turn, they will attack us.' . . . After I looked things over, I stood up and said to the nobles, the officials and the rest of the people, 'Don't be afraid of them. Remember the Lord, who is great and awesome, and fight for your families, your sons your daughters, your wives and your homes.' When our enemies heard that we were aware of their plot and that God had frustrated it, we all returned to the wall, each to our own work."

Nehemiah 4: 11-14, NIV

We praise You, O Great and Mighty God
You Who see all and know all
You Who are in all and through all.

We turn our face to You and are not afraid.

Lord,
You are great, You are awesome.

We are Your multicolored creation.

Lord,
You are great, You are awesome.

You Who have given us our sons and daughters, our families.

Lord,
You are great, You are awesome.

We will not fear the threats to attack us.

Lord, You are great, You are awesome.

Destroy and frustrate the plans of every opposer of justice and mercy.

Lord,
You are great, You are awesome.

We turn our back to every enemy who without cause attempts to end our work or the lives of image bearers.

Lord,
You are great, You are awesome.

Make Your vision ours, Your will, ours.
For we offer the care and completion of this work to You,
O, Mighty God.

You are great, You are awesome.

Hands Up
Hands Up

Lord, You are great, You are awesome.
We worship You with our hands raised up in praise.
Amen.

–MFW

PLEASURES

Don't you long to laugh
just for joy's sake?
Not in response
to anything you've
seen or heard,
but because it feels
so good to throw your
head back and let that
smile on the inside
run up your throat,
across your tongue
then out of your lips
into the most joyful,
ear-splitting laughter
anyone has ever heard.

Acts 17:28
    -MFW

ABOUT THE AUTHORS

Andrew W. Fitz (1895-1986) was the author of three poetry books, countless unpublished poems, and an inspirational booklet, "Try It." In the 1930s he built his own car and was a trademark and patent holder for several inventions. "A.W." as he was known, was the son of former slaves and a graduate of Kansas State College in Manhattan, Kansas. He served in the personnel department of the 65th Pioneer Infantry during World War I.

Born in Coffeyville, Kansas, he lived most of his adult life in Council Bluffs, Iowa. There he was active in civic affairs that involved the betterment of Black people. He served as president of the Council Bluffs NAACP, and lived his final years in Omaha, Nebraska.

—

Mari Fitz-Wynn is an experienced writer with nearly thirty years of writing expertise. She has published two books, *Take Heart* and *Connect the D.O.T.S.,* and has another one, *Anointed to Dream* in the works. She's published numerous articles in several magazines such as *A Woman's Heart and Soul,* the *National AG Woman's* magazine and the *Chattanooga Weekly*. She is the recipient of a United Arts Council literary grant and placed second in the Blue Ridge Mountain Christian Writers Conference Articles Competition, and she is a popular speaker. Her debut as a Poet has been a long time coming as she's steadied herself on the shoulders of her great-grandparents, grandparents, and her parents.

Though there have been small gains, the social landscape of this country looks very close to the one in which they lived, but with each succeeding generation, hope for positive change continues to grow.

AFTERWORD

What is a legacy, an inheritance? Things left for future generations—not just money or property but words, ideas, inspiration, and hope. Something to look back on, something to push us forward.

Our great-grandfather, Andrew Wilbert Fitz, was a Renaissance man, talented in multiple ways. He was a gifted writer and a genius inventor. You have read some of his words in this book. Our great-grandmother, his wife Beatrice Maddox Fitz, was a classically trained and highly gifted concert pianist. Together they both instilled in our mother's father—our beloved and greatly missed grandfather—a love of words and music that was, in turn, passed on to our mother, and now to us.

We inherit the family legacy of words, of music, of perseverance in the face of ignorance and trauma.

We never met our great-grandfather, he died just before great-granddaughter, Rooney was born, and though we did meet our great-grandmother when we were very young, our memories of her are faint. But we know that they dreamed for us, dreams for our success.

Much of who we are and the values we hold are a result of our predecessors, of their lives and their sacrifices. Clear-eyed and rich with hard-won wisdom, they sought to inspire by word and deed; their lives were living credits to what they endured and conquered.

A.W. Fitz's writings are about freedoms he never experienced. His poems are an outcry and a reproach. With words, he strained at the tethers, and his efforts crystallize our commitment to progress. *Progress within makes progress without*, writes our great-grandfather, and those words still resonate.

Here we stand, the light of freedom dim on our faces—a light we see imperfectly now, but which was even dimmer to the ancestors that strove against the shackles of bigotry, even bigotry found in their religion-otherwise a source of solace. *How long will prejudice be mixed with prayer?* our great-grandfather asks, and that question remains a relevant one.

The blood of poets and musicians, of the determined, unbowed, and unbroken, runs in our veins. Blood once drawn by the lash, chilled by the ugly racist stain on this nation, rose up to the thought of protest and equality and hope. That hope is ours.

And so, we become the legacies of those we never knew and of those who raised us. Our mother: vibrant, vital, powerful, and a poet. Our grandfather: an activist, a gifted and talented musician who loved us greatly. Our great-grandparents, literary and musically gifted, brilliant and bold.

We, their descendants, are not the summation of nor the conclusion to their legacies but something more striking still—their continuation. Their voices are not silent while we live.

-Rooney Lindelle Fitz Wynn and Keifer Anthony Fitz Wynn, Great-grandchildren of A.W. Fitz, and children of Mari Fitz-Wynn

www.ingramcontent.com/pod-product-compliance
Lightning Source LLC
Chambersburg PA
CBHW020333010526
44119CB00002B/44